SPOTLIGHT ON NATIVE AMERICANS

CHOCTAW

Ada Quinlivan

New York

Published in 2016 by The Rosen Publishing Group, Inc.
29 East 21st Street, New York, NY 10010

First Edition

Book Design: Samantha DeMartin
Material reviewed by: Donald A. Grinde, Jr., Professor of Transnational/American Studies at the State University of New York at Buffalo.

Photo Credits: Cover Roger Zettler/Daily Star/AP Images; p. 5 François Bernard/Wikimedia Commons; p. 7 Jody Dingle/Shutterstock.com; pp. 9, 10, 16–17 MPI/Archive Photos/Getty Images; p. 13 Visual Studies Workshop/Archive Photos/Getty Images; p. 15 Natalie Maynor/Flickr.com; p. 19 Ditch Fisher/Wikimedia Commons; p. 20 George Catlin/Wikimedia Commons; p. 22 Xasartha/Wikimedia Commons; p. 23 English Wikipedia/Wikimedia Commons; p. 25 (inset) Fort Worth Star-Telegram/Tribune News Service/Getty Images; p. 25 (main) Kevin Jackson, AMC/US Army; p. 26 Kodi Tanner/Flickr.com; p. 27 Robert Alexander/Archive Photos/Getty Images; p. 28 U.S. Department of the Interior/Flickr.com; p. 29 Saul Loeb/AFP/Getty Images.

Library of Congress Cataloging-in-Publication Data

Quinlivan, Ada, author.
 Choctaw / Ada Quinlivan.
    pages cm. — (Spotlight on Native Americans)
 Includes index.
 ISBN 978-1-5081-4110-5 (pbk.)
 ISBN 978-1-5081-4111-2 (6 pack)
 ISBN 978-1-5081-4113-6 (library binding)
 1. Choctaw Indians—History—Juvenile literature. 2. Choctaw Indians—Social life and customs—
Juvenile literature. I. Title.
 E99.C8Q85 2016
 305.897'387—dc23

                              2015031624

Manufactured in the United States of America

CPSIA Compliance Information: Batch #BW16PK: For Further Information contact Rosen Publishing, New York, New York at
1-800-237-9932

CONTENTS

THE BEGINNINGS OF THE CHOCTAW

CHAPTER 1

The Choctaw people have overcome centuries of hardship to become a strong, unified nation that has a bright future. Today, there are about 200,000 members of the Choctaw Nation of Oklahoma and nearly 10,000 members of the Mississippi Band of Choctaw Indians. Their life after European contact was changed forever, but the Choctaw strived to maintain their important traditions and ways of life.

The Choctaw are one of the more than 500 native groups in the United States and 600 in Canada. The ancestors of Native Americans likely traveled to North America on a land bridge from Asia. This happened during an **ice age** around 12,000 years ago when sea levels were low because water was locked in ice. As hunters and gatherers, they were looking for food. Instead they found a whole new world.

Once they arrived in North America, the first people began to spread throughout the Americas. However, they didn't migrate, or move, together—they split into smaller groups. The groups developed ways of life based on where they settled. Some remained hunters and gatherers. Others grew crops and were able to settle in one place and form lasting communities.

The Choctaw people eventually settled in the southeastern United States, on land that's now mostly part of the state of Mississippi. Weather there is often very hot for much of the year. The Choctaw's environment, or surroundings, greatly affected their way of life.

ENCOUNTERING THE EUROPEANS

CHAPTER 3

The first interaction between the Choctaw and Europeans happened around 1540. They met Spanish explorer Hernando de Soto's expedition—a meeting that ended in a bloody fight. However, relations with the Europeans weren't as bad as they were between the Europeans and many other Native American groups. By the 1700s, Europeans had officially started exploring and settling near the Choctaw, and the two groups began trading with each other. The Choctaw were peaceful and willing to work with the Europeans.

Over time, the Choctaw's willingness to coexist with white settlers made them one of America's "five civilized tribes." These also included the Seminole, Cherokee, Creek, and Chickasaw. The Choctaw adopted many white ways, including their dress. They also married white settlers, and some accepted Christianity. They were **allies** with the French during wars between the French and English settlers during the 1700s. This caused them to lose land after the French and Indian War, which occurred between 1754 and 1763. The victorious British, angry with French allies, took Choctaw land, forcing them to move west.

Unfortunately, that was only the beginning of the Choctaw losing their land. Over the next century, they'd be forced farther and farther out of their home territory.

This painting shows how a traditional Choctaw camp along the Mississippi River might have looked.

LOSING THEIR LAND

CHAPTER 4

After the American Revolution, the new United States government wanted to **assimilate** Native Americans into white society. That meant Native Americans giving up their traditional ways of life. The Choctaw had already been living in peace with white settlers, however, and had already adopted some of

their ways, which is called acculturation. As a peaceful people, the Choctaw didn't want to fight the U.S. government.

When the time came to form new boundaries on their territory, the Choctaw signed treaties, or formal agreements. The Treaty of Hopewell in 1786 established peace between the United States and the Choctaw people. For a while, it seemed as if peace were possible. However, the U.S. government drew up new treaties that changed the borders. The Choctaw lost millions of acres of territory, until they were left with little land.

In 1830, the United States claimed the remaining part of Choctaw territory for the growing country. The Choctaw were to be relocated west to Indian Territory in what is today the state of Oklahoma. This journey was made on foot with little food or water. It became known as the Trail of Tears, and the Choctaw were the first Native Americans to walk it.

Nearly 2,500 Choctaws died on the Trail of Tears. Not only did they have to leave their homeland, but they were headed for an unknown future.

INDIAN TERRITORY

CHAPTER 5

The Choctaw had to adjust to the new environment in Oklahoma. Although they'd lost their home, the Choctaw were willing to rebuild in the new land. The first thing they did was build a church and school. For the next 60 years, the Choctaw rebuilt their culture in their new land. They not only helped themselves, but helped others, too. When they heard about the potato **famine** happening in Ireland from 1845 to 1852, the Choctaw scraped together $170 to send there.

Despite their charity and peaceful ways, the Choctaw had their land stolen once again. In 1889, white settlers began coming to the Oklahoma Territory. White settlers to Oklahoma—called homesteaders—hurt, murdered, and stole from the Choctaw. In 1907, Oklahoma became a state, and the Choctaw were forced to become U.S. citizens, which greatly limited their ability for self-government.

These Choctaw women are weaving baskets in Oklahoma in the early 1900s.

Beginning in the 1940s, the United States tried to further strip Native American governments of their power. The U.S. government wanted to limit the rights of native governments so that Native Americans could fully enter white society.

CHOCTAW TRADITIONS AND CULTURE

CHAPTER 6

Despite the hardships they faced, the Choctaw found ways to continue their traditional ways of life. Over time, some things have changed, while others have stayed the same.

In the past, the Choctaw lived in **thatched** dwellings in villages surrounded by cornfields. Men were hunters. They used blowguns, which were long, hollow canes through which a dart could be blown. They also used rabbit sticks, which were hammer-like sticks that could be thrown to kill an animal. Meanwhile, women took care of farming, cooking, and raising the children. Choctaw mothers carried their babies on **cradleboards** so they could work and watch their children at the same time.

Choctaw men wore a strip of cloth around their waist called a breechcloth, while women wore skirts. Clothes were usually made out of deerskin. Like many native groups, the Choctaw sometimes wore moccasins, though they often walked barefoot. By the 1800s, the Choctaw began using European-style clothing. Men wore pants and a shirt, or an outfit of deerskin. Women wore cotton shirts and skirts, or dresses. For special ceremonies, Choctaw women wore bright, colorful, hand-sewn dresses with ruffles and a white apron.

These dancers perform a traditional dance at the Choctaw Indian Fair in Mississippi.

CHOCTAW CREATIONS

CHAPTER 7

The Choctaw have kept their history and culture alive through traditional crafts and pastimes. They play traditional music and tell traditional legends. These legends often have animals as their main characters, which shows how important nature is to Choctaw culture.

The Choctaw once used the long, hollow sticks of swamp cane to weave strong baskets. They also used swamp cane to make their houses. Once the Choctaw were

removed to Oklahoma, they no longer had swamp cane to build and craft with. Many focused instead on beadwork, crafting beads into artwork, jewelry, and ceremonial clothing. These art forms are still practiced today.

The Choctaw still enjoy traditional sports, such as *toli*, which is a stickball game much like lacrosse. Choctaw ball games once had hundreds of players and even more people watching. The Choctaw also enjoyed playing a game similar to dice, using beans, seeds, or corn.

Food is a big part of traditional Choctaw celebrations and ceremonies. Traditional Choctaw food often involves corn, as that was their main crop. Choctaws still make fried corn, corn fritters, and corn chowder.

This artwork shows Choctaw men playing their traditional stickball game around 1835. Hundreds of men would take part in each game.

CHOCTAW CREATION LEGEND

CHAPTER 8

The Choctaw have many legends they've passed down for hundreds of years. Perhaps the most important legend they have is how the Choctaw came to be. There are several accounts of this legend.

One account says that Nanih Waiya was the birthplace of humankind. According to the legend, from this mound came the Muscogees. They laid on the mound to dry in the sun, and then they moved east. The Cherokee then stumbled out of Nanih Waiya, and they they also sunned themselves. They smoked tobacco and accidentally set the woods on fire, removing the path the Muscogees took. The Cherokee had no choice but to make their own path, so they went north.

Next, the Chickasaw people came forth from Nanih Waiya. They dried in the sun and then set out to find the others. They followed the Cherokee's trail and found them. They settled near the Cherokee people in the north.

The Choctaw were the last group to come from Nanih Waiya. They left the mound, went out into the sun to dry, and then decided not to move forward. Instead, they settled right near Nanih Waiya.

Today, you can visit Nanih Waiya Mound and Village in Winston County, Mississippi, to see the mound that held so much importance to early Choctaw **culture**.

BELIEFS OF THE CHOCTAW

CHAPTER 9

The Choctaw accepted Christianity when the Europeans came to North America. However, before that, they had their own strong spiritual beliefs. Many have been passed down and still affect Choctaw culture today.

The Choctaw believed performing certain dances would please the spiritual world and affect nature. This painting shows a Choctaw Eagle Dance.

The Choctaw believed in both good and evil **supernatural** beings. The greatest supernatural being was the Superior Being. The Choctaw believed the Superior Being, known as Nanapesa or Nanishtahullo Chito, watched them through a hole in the sky—the sun. Fire represented the sun, so it was very important to the people.

Another good supernatural being was Ohoyo Osh Chishba, who introduced the Choctaw to corn. Kowi Anuk Asha were little creatures who taught Choctaw doctors about medicine. Evil supernatural beings included Nalusa Chito, a being that's like the devil. Other evil beings captured, frightened, and harmed people.

Traditional Choctaw placed their doctors and prophets very high in society and believed they had a bond with the spiritual world. Prophets, who were called *hopaii*, guided people based on what the spirits told them. They were believed to use their power to make rain. A chief would plan ceremonies and celebrations, the greatest being the Green Corn Ceremony. The Choctaw gave thanks for the corn and participated in ceremonial dancing.

TODAY'S CHOCTAW: THE MISSISSIPPI BAND

CHAPTER 10

The white settlers weren't successful in removing all the Choctaw from their land in the Southeast. In fact, some hid or refused to leave, while others passed as white so they didn't have

to move. They formed the Mississippi Band of Choctaw Indians. Unlike those removed to Oklahoma, this band was able to stay in their native environment, which helped keep their traditional culture alive.

Today, there are about 10,000 members of the Mississippi Band of Choctaw Indians. They live on the Choctaw Indian **Reservation**. This 35,000-acre (14,164 ha) territory is home to eight communities, including Bogue Chitto, Bogue Homa, Crystal Ridge, Conehatta, Pearl River, Standing Pine, Red Water, and Tucker.

The Mississippi Band of Choctaw Indians is the only native group in Mississippi that's recognized by the U.S. government. They received federal recognition in 1945. The first female Choctaw chief was Chief Phyliss J. Anderson, and she was elected in 2011. The Mississippi Band of Chocktaw Indians has the largest unified reservation school system in the country. It features educational programs for children and adults alike. The reservation has its own health department, which provides health services to the Choctaw living there.

Staying in Mississippi allowed the Mississippi Band of Choctaw Indians to keep many of their traditions alive.

TODAY'S CHOCTAW: CHOCTAW NATION OF OKLAHOMA

CHAPTER 11

The Choctaw in Oklahoma faced many injustices in the early 1900s. The U.S. government did all it could to destroy the Choctaw government and culture. Luckily, the American Indian Movement (AIM) was founded in 1968. In the decades that followed, AIM fought for rights for native peoples, including the Choctaw.

In 1971, the Choctaw Nation of Oklahoma was able to hold its first election of a chief in over 60 years. That same decade, the Indian Self-Determination and Education Assistance Act gave the Choctaw the ability to communicate with the U.S. government about services they needed. The Choctaw people **ratified** the Choctaw Nation **Constitution** on July 9, 1983. It broke the nation's government into three branches, much like the U.S. government. The Tribal **Council** was established to make laws, approve budgets, and make decisions on Choctaw property. The Choctaw people elect the 12 members of this council.

The Choctaw Nation has a strong history of serving in the United States military. During World War I, the Choctaw in the U.S. Army developed a code based on their language. They were called "code talkers," and they helped the U.S. forces win important battles by communicating through code.

Many Choctaw risked their life for the United States during World War I, even though the government had taken their land. This is the Choctaw Nation Color Guard.

A STRONG COMMUNITY

CHAPTER 12

The Choctaw Nation is a proud, self-governed nation that has many successful businesses and a strong community. Their businesses include seven **casinos**, 12 smoke shops, and 13 travel plazas. Choctaw Nation businesses employ more than 6,000 people, and many employees are members of the nation. The Choctaw Nation is the largest employer in southeastern Oklahoma. The money that's made from businesses is put back into the community. It pays for education, housing, and health-care programs for the Choctaw.

Just as the Choctaw gave money to those suffering from the potato famine, they're still known for their charity today. In 2015, the Choctaw Nation was awarded the Beacon Award, which recognized the nation's aid to military **veterans**. The nation

helps provide free flights for wounded veterans and their loved ones.

Chahta Anumpa Aiikhvna, or the School of Choctaw Language, works to keep their traditional language alive and pass it to the next generation. Students follow a special educational program that also covers the history and culture of their people.

The Choctaw Nation has many notable and talented members, including artist Marcus Amerman. He uses beads and glass to make his artwork, and he also does performance art. Amerman made this beaded artwork to sell at the Santa Fe Indian Market in Santa Fe, New Mexico.

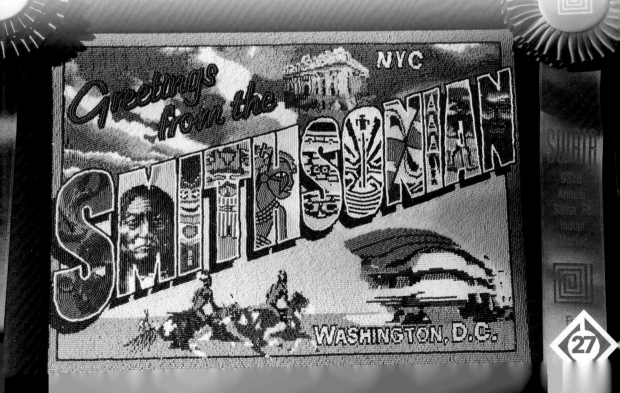

A BRIGHT FUTURE

CHAPTER 13

Today, despite many successes, the Choctaw continue to face many of the same hardships faced by other native peoples in Oklahoma, including **poverty**, unacceptable housing, alcohol abuse, and crime. The potential of the  Choctaw Nation hasn't gone unnoticed, however. In 2013, President Obama announced the Promise Zone initiative. In five select zones—including the Choctaw Nation—the local and federal governments partnered with local businesses and communities to increase education, economic security, housing, and jobs. The Choctaw Nation developed a list of plans to benefit their community, including improving job skills, improving the economy through Choctaw-owned businesses, improving education, and using natural and cultural resources to grow the economy. This is a great step forward for the Choctaw Nation.

The Choctaw people have a rich history, from their beginnings as a farming society in southeastern United States until today. Although they valued peace and trade, the Choctaw faced many injustices and were removed from their homeland. However, in the past few decades, the Choctaw people have had great success in business, and hold great promise to grow and prosper in the future.

President Barack Obama speaks at a high school in Oklahoma about the economic promise of the Choctaw Nation.

GLOSSARY

ally: One of two or more people or groups who work together.

assimilate: To cause a person or group to become part of a different society or country.

casino: A building where gambling takes place.

constitution: The basic laws and principles of a nation or state that outline the powers of the government and the rights of the people.

council: A group of people who are chosen to make rules, laws, or decisions about something.

cradleboard: A portable cradle made of a board or frame onto which a baby is secured with blankets or binding.

culture: The beliefs and ways of life of a group of people.

descendant: A relative of someone from an earlier time.

famine: A situation in which many people do not have enough to eat.

ice age: A period during which temperatures fall worldwide and large areas are covered with glaciers.

poverty: The state of being poor.

ratify: To formally approve something.

reservation: Land set aside by the government for a specific Native American group or groups to live on.

supernatural: Unable to be explained by science or the laws of nature.

thatched: Having a roof made of dried plant material.

veteran: Someone who has served in the military.

FOR MORE INFORMATION

BOOKS

De Capua, Sarah. *The Choctaw.* Tarrytown, NY: Cavendish Square
    Publishing, 2009.

Gibson, Karen Bush. *Native American History for Kids: With
    21 Activities.* Chicago, IL: Chicago Review Press, 2010.

Gray-Kanatiiosh, Barbara A. *Choctaw.* Edina, MN: ABDO
    Publishing, 2007.

WEBSITES

Due to the changing nature of Internet links, PowerKids Press has
developed an online list of websites related to the subject of this book.
This site is updated regularly. Please use this link to access the list:
www.powerkidslinks.com/sona/choc

INDEX